How To Buy State Tax Lien Properties In Utah Real Estate

Get Tax Lien Certificates, Tax Lien And Deed Homes For Sale In Utah

by

Christian Mahoney

Get Massive Money for Real Estate Now!

1. Private Lending and Hard Money (Text Manual) (similar guides have sold for $1,500.00 alone)

2. Real Estate Investing Guide (Text Guide)

3. Goldmine Government Grants (Video Training Program)

4. Residential Government Grant Programs (Video Training Program)

5. Commercial Government Grant Programs (Video Training Program)

6. Creative Financing (Video Training Program)

7. Expert Credit Repair (Video Training Program)

8. Million Dollar Video Marketing (Video Training Program)

9. Customer List Building (Video Training Program)

10. Massive Web Site Traffic (Video Training Program)

11. SEO Marketing (Video Training Program)

12. Bonus 1000 Package!!!

Just Hit the Link Below Right Now!!!

Don't Wait....You'll Wait Your Life Away...

http://www.BrianSMahoney.com

Get Our Massive Money Complete Internet Marketing Video Training Program at:

(Zero Cost Internet Marketing complete 142 video series)

$1,997 Megasized Money Making Marketing Program

ONLY $67 !!!!

https://goo.gl/Qed1dY

**Join Our VIP Mailing List and Get FREE Money Making Training Videos! Then Start Making Money within 24 hours!
Plus if you join our Mailing list you can get Revised and New Edition versions of your book free!**

And Notifications of other FREE Offers!

Just Hit/Type in the Link Below

https://mahoneyproducts.wixsite.com/win1

About the Author

Christian Mahoney worked hard in the Thomas Nelson College Bookstore before going on to earn a Degree in Science from the school. He also attended Hampton University and went on to earn a B.S. degree in Education from Radford University in Radford Virginia. He is currently a candidate for his Masters Degree from Old Dominion University in Norfolk Virginia.

He excelled in school earning a certificate of Excellence from Harkness Hall Hampton University, and making the Dean's list at Radford University.

In High School he was a shooting guard and a defensive star on the Gloucester High School Basketball team.

Christian enjoys attending blockbuster movies, great dining and being around family and friends.

He learned about business growing up working for his father's company on weekends and found a love for books while working in the campus bookstore.

The experience of working in the college bookstore helped Christian to see the joy that people got from having a book to educate and enrich their lives. After getting a degree in Education he decided to produce a book that educates and helps people. It has been a great joy in his life.

Copyright © 2017 Christian Mahoney
All rights reserved.

DEDICATION

This book is dedicated to my Father Brian Mahoney.

ACKNOWLEDGMENTS

I WOULD LIKE TO ACKNOWLEDGE ALL THE HARD WORK OF THE MEN AND WOMEN OF THE UNITED STATES MILITARY, WHO RISK THEIR LIVES ON A DAILY BASIS, TO MAKE THE WORLD A SAFER PLACE.

Disclaimer

This book was written as a guide to starting a business. As with any other high yielding action, starting a business has a certain degree of risk. This book is not meant to take the place of accounting, legal, financial or other professional advice. If advice is needed in any of these fields, you are advised to seek the services of a professional.

While the author has attempted to make the information in this book as accurate as possible, no guarantee is given as to the accuracy or currency of any individual item. Laws and procedures related to business are constantly changing.

Therefore, in no event shall Christian Mahoney, the author of this book be liable for any special, indirect, or consequential damages or any damages whatsoever in connection with the use of the information herein provided.

All Rights Reserved

No part of this book may be used or reproduced in any manner whatsoever without the written permission of the author.

Table of Contents

Chapter 1   Tax Sale Property Overview

Chapter 2   Finding Tax Sale Property in Utah

Chapter 3   How To Finance Real Estate

Chapter 4   Goldmine Government Grants

Chapter 5   How to reach a billion people with YouTube Video Marketing

Chapter 6   How to write a expert business plan

Chapter 7   How to set goals and stay focus

Chapter 8   Real Estate Terms

Chapter 1

Tax Sale Property Overview

Tax Sale Property Overview

Buying Tax Lien and Tax Deed Properties

What are Government Property Tax Sales?

A government property tax sale is a public auction that the government uses to recover delinquent real estate property taxes.

Why does the county have the public auction?

If a propety owner can not pay the delinquent taxes, the public auction gives the county the oppurtunity to recoup the back taxes owned, and recover any penalties and interest due. It puts a sense of urgency on the property owner and gives those that have the money to pay the taxes an opportunity to get a property at a discounted rate.

Tax Sale Property Overview

What is a Internet public auction tax sale?

By using the internet to hold a public auction, counties are able to have bids placed using a computer, and widen the potential number of buyers.

Who can participate in the online public auctions?

Anyone who registers and then places a pre-bid deposit can participate in online auctions.

What is a Tax Deed?

A tax deed is a document used to show title to real estate after the property has been sold at a public auction, by the government in charge of collecting property taxes.

Tax Sale Property Overview

What is a tax deed public auction sale?

A tax deed sale is a public auciton for property that has a tax default. The deeds to the property are sold to the highest bidder. Usually the bidding starts at a combination of the penalty fees, interest charges and the delinquent taxes.

Tax Deed states are:

- Alaska
- Arkansas
- California
- Connecticut
- Delaware
- Florida
- Georgia
- Hawaii
- Idaho
- Kansas

Tax Sale Property Overview

Maine

Michigan

Missouri

Nevada

New Hampshire

New Mexico

New York

North Carolina

North Dakota

Ohio

Oklahoma

Oregon

Pennsylvania

Rhode Island

South Dakota

Tennessee

Utah

Tax Sale Property Overview

Virginia

Washington

Wisconsin

What is a Tax Lien Sale?

A tax lien sale is a public auction authorized by the state government for tax liens of real property. Tax liens are sold for the amount of a combination of the penalty fees, interest charges and the delinquent taxes. You do not own the house when you purchase a tax lien. You own the right to get paid all of your money back, with interest after a set time period that varies with each state. The interest rate also varies with each state.

Tax Sale Property Overview

List of Tax Lien Certificate States:

Alabama

Arizona

Colorado

Florida

Illinois

Iowa

Indiana

Kentucky

Louisiana

Maryland

Massachusetts

Mississippi

Montana

Nebraska

New Jersey

New York

Tax Sale Property Overview

Ohio

South Carolina

Vermont

Washington DC

West Virginia

Wyoming

Tax lien and Tax deed property sales are a great way for an investor to either earn interest on their money or to get a property for pennies on the dollar.

Chapter 2

Finding Real Estate in Utah

Quick & Easy Access to Foreclosure Real Estate

Getting Started

When Investing in Utah first you have to determine what county you want to purchase in. To help you decide, below is a list of all counties in Utah with their population and square miles. After the list of all the counties, you get a Goldmine Rolodex of web site address of Wholesale Government Tax Sale Properties and More!

Utah Counties | Population | Square Miles

Utah Counties	Population	Square Miles
Salt Lake County	1,029,665	742
Utah County	516,564	2,003
Davis County	306,479	299
Weber County	231,236	576
Washington County	138,115	2,426
Cache County	112,656	1,165
Tooele County	58,218	6,941
Box Elder County	49,975	5,746
Iron County	46,163	3,297
Summit County	36,324	1,872
Uintah County	32,588	4,480

Utah Counties	Population	Square Miles
Sanpete County	27,882	1,590
Wasatch County	23,530	1,176
Carbon County	21,403	1,478
Sevier County	20,802	1,911
Duchesne County	18,607	3,241
San Juan County	14,746	7,820
Millard County	12,503	6,572
Emery County	10,976	4,462
Juab County	10,246	3,392
Morgan County	9,469	609
Grand County	9,225	3,672
Kane County	7,125	3,990
Beaver County	6,629	2,590
Garfield County	5,172	5,175
Wayne County	2,589	2,461
Rich County	2,264	1,029
Piute County	1,556	758
Daggett County	1,059	697

Utah

As of the writting of this book, all of these websites are up and running. From time to time some will change their address. If a site does not come up sometimes using the root of the address works. For example if www.mystate.gov/wholesaleproperty does not work. Just go with www.mystate.gov/

Utah Tax Sale/Foreclosure PROPERTIES

Utah County

http://www.utahcounty.gov/taxsale/index.html

Salt Lake County

http://slco.org/auditor/tax-sale/

Locate Statewide Utah Properties

MLS

http://www.mls.com/search/utah.mvc

Utah Real Estate Foreclosures with links to different cities on the landing page.

REALTOR

https://goo.gl/NxFHCj

Links to Utah real estate properties by county and city.

UNITED STATES REAL ESTATE INFO

http://www.statelocalgov.net/50states-tax-authorities.cfm

http://www.brbpub.com/free-public-records/

www.RealAuction.com

www.GrantStreet.com

Locate Nationwide Foreclosure Auction Properties

http://www.bid4assets.com/

Bid4assets is an amazing website for quickly finding investment property. The landing page has a map of the United States and you can just move your mouse pointer over the state you are interested in to see if they have any property in their database.

Here are just a few of assets you can target on this site!

* County Tax Sales

* Bank Owned Property

* US Marshal

* Real Estate

* Coins

* $1 No Reserve Homes

Locate Nationwide Foreclosure Auction Properties

Http://www.realauction.com

Real Auction is another great website for instant access to property information.

Once on the landing page click "client sites".

They have 4 categories of information.

* Tax Liens Auctions

* Tax Deeds Applications

* Foreclosure and Tax Deed Auctions

* Tax Deed Management

Then chose from the states and counties that appear, that they have auction information.

CHAPTER 3

FINANCING REAL ESTATE

8 Realistic Ways to Finance Real Estate

FINANCING REAL ESTATE

Welcome to Expert financing. I am going to show you several realistic ways to finance real estate. You are going to learn how to finance real estate with.

* VA LOANS

* PARTNERS

* INVESTMENT CLUBS

* CREDIT CARDS

* CORPORATE CREDIT

* EQUITY

* SELLER FINANCE

* HARD MONEY LENDERS

* AND FINALLY I SHOW YOU THE MONEY$!!

USING A VA LOAN

According to the web sites www.benefits.va.gov and www.military.com the current VA Loan amount is a whopping $417,000! What a lot of veterans don't know is that you can use that money to purchase not only your home, but investment properties. That is how I started my investing career. Purchasing multiple homes using my VA Loan.

FINANCING REAL ESTATE

Even if you are not a veteran, you can still partner up with one, who still has some money left on his or her VA LOAN.

If you are a Veteran, you will need to obtain a copy of your DD 214 and VA Form 26-1880 Request for a Certificate of Eligibility.

PARTNERS

This is another way I purchased a home. At the time I worked for the United States Postal Service. I had already purchased plenty of homes, so many of the workers were aware I had successfully invested in real estate. At break time I went around and ask people to partner up with me. I had multiple people offer to go in as a partner. I choose one and that house we rehabbed and flipped just two months after purchasing it. To this day it was the biggest gross profit on one deal, I have had. True I had to split it with my partner, but I would rather have half of something than all of nothing.

Having the combined resources of two people can be a great benefit, but it is not without it's challenges. If you are going to use a partner, no matter how close you are...GET EVERY THING IN WRITING.

FINANCING REAL ESTATE

Having a partner can dramatically increase the chance of a Bank lending money as well as having someone to split the work on rehabbing, should you decide to save money and make repairs yourself. But all this must be spelled out BEFORE you enter into a Agreement/Contract and purchase a home.

It helps if the person is like minded and understands the risks and benefits of investing, and truly understands the return on investment of a particular deal.

REAL ESTATE INVESTMENT CLUBS

Real estate investment clubs are groups that meet locally and allow investors and other professionals to network and learn. They can provide extremely useful information for both the novice and expert real estate investor. A top real estate club can provide a great forum to network, learn about reputable contractors, brokers, realtors, lawyers, accountants and other professionals. On the other hand, there are many real estate clubs designed to sell you. They bring in "gurus" who sell either on stage or at the back of the room, and as a result, the clubs typically profit to the tune of %50 of the sale price of the product, bootcamp, or training that is pitched.

FINANCING REAL ESTATE

I have purchased a ton of real estate books and real estate courses. Carlton Sheets, Dave Del Dotto, The Mylands, Seminar courses and much much more. I am not against any club bringing in a speaker who has a course. However I think there should be transparency to the members of the club.

There is certainly value in the networking that may come at one of these groups. But attend working to attain your goals and not necessarily the club's goal to sell you something. Some times both are the same thing. As a rule I usually leave debit cards at home the first time I attend an event. If there is a seller there with a "This day only offer" then I won't feel pressured to purchase. Plus most sellers can be convinced to sell at the discount offer price at a later time when you have had a chance to come down off the "sense of urgency emotional pitch" .

CREDIT CARDS

When using a credit card in real estate you must really do your homework on the deal. Dan Kennedy a world famous marketer once said "always stack the numbers in your favor". That's how you use a credit card. Look at the return on investment as compared to the long term cost of using a credit card and it's interest. Also I would recommend buying low cost homes that you can purchase and own free and clear.

FINANCING REAL ESTATE

No Mortgage Payment!!! My last 2 homes I have purchased have been cash deals. One home cost $1,500 and the other about $7,000. The first was a government property from HUD and the 2nd From a Bank. These institutions are unemotional about real estate and simply view a property as a non performing asset. The 2nd home was 4 bedrooms, 1 1/2 bath and a basement located in a farming community and came with a 2 car garage/shed and .6 acre(that is the size of a NFL football field) of land.

Later in this book I will show you how to find plenty of houses with amazing below wholesale prices and a formula for almost always finding a great deal.

CORPORATE CREDIT

Many people set up corporations to buy and sell real estate as an additional protection against liabilities. Other's create a corporation to mask personal involvement in property transfers and public records. Regardless of the use of a corporation, you can buy real estate with corporate credit as an alternative to using your own cash or IRA. By capitalizing on the credit rating of your corporation, you can buy real estate and build your corporate holdings portfolio.

FINANCING REAL ESTATE

Just remember that you can set up your corporation in a state that favors you the most for your real estate deals. Do your research. Most people like Delaware and Nevada, but you will have to decide if your home state or any other state is best for you and your business.

CURRENT EQUITY

Using the equity in your home for real estate investing is another way you can finance properties. You might use the money for a down payment or it may only be enough to cover the cost of some rehab repairs.

If you stick to the low cost home formula, you may have enough to purchase the entire house. A house is an investment that should appreciate in value as well as give a great ROI (Return On Investment). Whether you decide to flip the property or rent it out for positive cashflow.

If you have equity and it's not doing anything, then you may decide to make it a "performing asset" and use it as part of your real estate finance program.

FINANCING REAL ESTATE

SELLER FINANCING

Seller finance is where the seller of a free and clear property becomes your bank along with being the seller.

Advantages:

You get to purchase the property on terms that may be more beneficial for you. Seller gets monthly payments and the benefit of treating the sale as an installment sale thus allowing them to defer any capital gains taxes that may be due.

Disadvantages:

You may be locked into a mortgage with a pre-payment penalty or may not be able to resell the property immediately. This strategy is typically not meant for flipping but can definitely be used for that purpose if structured correctly.

Seller Finance is a known way to finance a property. That is why I have presented it in this book. But it is my least favorite because you now have a lingering relationship with your property. Your ability to make decisions regarding the property is limited and for that reason, I would don't go this route. However, like all types of financing, you have to ask yourself, "is the deal worth it."

FINANCING REAL ESTATE

I also prefer to work alone, but when a great deal came along, I sought out a partner to make it happen. Risk is usually relative to potential profit.

HARD MONEY LENDERS

A hard money lender is usually a individual or company that lends money for investment of a secured by the investment property.

Advantages:

Less red tape to get the money. You are dealing with people who understand the real estate investment business.

Disadvantage:

This is not a long term loan. The lender wants a return on investment, usually within a few months, a a year, or a few years. The interest rate on the loan is much higher than usual conventional banks.

Using hard money has a higher risk because the return on investment is due quicker. Therefore it is good idea not to use a Hard Money Lender, until you have a great deal of experience and confidence in being able to produce a return on investment.

SHOWING YOU THE MONEY

www.businessfinance.com (4,000 sources of money!)

www.advanceamericaproperty.com

http://www.cashadvanceloan.com/

www.brookviewfinancial.com

www.commercialfundingcorp.com

www.dhlc.com
(hard money for the Texas area)

www.equity-funding.com

www.bankofamerica.com

www.carolinahardmoney.com
(for real estate investors in North and South Carolina)

www.fpfloans.com

Chapter 4

Small Business Grants

How to write a Winning Grant Proposal

Small Business Grants

Government grants. Many people either don't believe government grants exist or they don't think they would ever be able to get government grant money.

First lets make one thing clear. Government grant money is **YOUR MONEY**. Government money comes from taxes paid by residents of this country. Depending on what state you live in, you are paying taxes on almost everything....Property tax for your house. Property tax on your car. Taxes on the things you purchase in the mall, or at the gas station. Taxes on your gasoline, the food you buy etc.

So get yourself in the frame of mind that you are not a charity case or too proud to ask for help, because billionaire companies like GM, Big Banks and most of Corporate America is not hesitating to get their share of **YOUR MONEY**!

There are over two thousand three hundred (2,300) Federal Government Assistance Programs. Some are loans but many are formula grants and project grants. To see all of the programs available go to:

http://www.CFDA.gov

WRITING A GRANT PROPOSAL

The Basic Components of a Proposal

There are eight basic components to creating a solid proposal package:

1. The proposal summary;

2. Introduction of organization;

3. The problem statement   (or needs assessment);

4. Project objectives;

5. Project methods or design;

6. Project evaluation;

7. Future funding; and

8. The project budget.

The Proposal Summary

The Proposal Summary is an outline of the project goals and objectives. Keep the Proposal Summary short and to the point. No more that 2 or 3 paragraphs. Put it at the beginning the proposal.

Introduction

The Introduction portion of your grant proposal presents you and your business as a credible applicant and organization.

Highlight the accomplishments of your organization from all sources: newspaper or online articles etc. Include a biography of key members and leaders. State the goals and philosophy of the company.

The Problem Statement

The problem statement makes clear the problem you are going to solve(maybe reduce homelessness). Make sure to use facts. State who and how those affected will benefits from solving the problem. State the exact manner in how you will solve the problem.

Project Objectives

The Project Objectives section of your grant proposal focuses on the Goals and Desired outcome.

Make sure to indentify all objectives and how you are going to reach these objectives. The more statistics you can find to support your objectives the better. Make sure to put in realistic objectives. You may be judged on how well you accomplish what you said you intended to do.

Program Methods and Design

The program methods and design section of your grant proposal is a detailed plan of action.

> What resources are going to be used.
>
> What staff in going to be needed.
>
> System development
>
> Create a Flow Chart of project features.
>
> Explain what will be achieved.
>
> Try to produce evidence of what will be achieved.
>
> Make a diagram of program design.

Evaluation

There is product evaluation and process evaluation. The product evaluation deals with the result that relate to the project and how well the project has met it's objectives.

The process evaluation deals with how the project was conducted, how did it line up the original stated plan and the overall effectiveness of the different aspects of the plan.

Evaluations can start at anytime during the project or at the project's conclusion. It is advised to submit a evaluation design at the start of a project.

It looks better if you have collected convincing data before and during the program.

If evaluation design is not presented at the beginning that might encourage a critical review of the program design.

Future Funding

The Future Funding part of the grant proposal should have long term project planning past the grant period.

Budget

Utilities, rental equipment, staffing, salary, food, transportation, phone bills and insurance are just some of the things to include in the budget.

A well constructed budget accounts for every penny.

A complete guide for government grants is available at the website link below.

https://www.cfda.gov/downloads/CFDA.GOV_Public_User_Guide_v2.0.pdf

The guide can also be accessed at the very bottom of every page of the https://www.cfda.gov/ website.

Other sources of Government Funding

You can get General Small Business loans from the government. Go to the Small Business Administration for more information.

SBA Microloan Program

The Microloan program provides loans of up to $50,000 with the average loan being $13,000.

https://www.sba.gov/

A Few Current Commercial Real Estate Grant/Loan Programs

Program Number: 10.415

Program Name: Rural Rental Housing Loans

Department: Department of Agriculture

Assistance: Grants - Direct Loans

Program Number: 10.438

Program Name: Section 538 Rural Rental

Department: Department of Agriculture

Assistance: Guaranteed Loans

Program Number: 14.191

Program Name: Multifamily Housing

Department: HUD

Assistance: Project Grants

A Few Current Commercial Real Estate Grant/Loan Programs

Program Number: 14.314

Program Name: Assisted Living Conversion

Department: HUD

Assistance: Project Grants

Program Number: 14.326

Program Name: Rental Assistance 811

Department: HUD

Assistance: Project Grants

Program Number: 14.329

Program Name: HUD Multifamily PSF Pilot

Department: HUD

Assistance: Direct Payments for Specified Use

Chapter 5
YouTube Video Marketing

YouTube Video Marketing Overview

Million Dollar Video Marketing

When you read the title of this book you may have thought the term "Million Dollar" was hyperbole. However the beauty of video marketing is that it can be done for free, and that there really are several people who make millions of dollars just on their YouTube video's alone. Meaning that they allow ads to be placed on them and they get paid a portion of what google gets from businesses that runs the ads.

Since they are only getting a portion of what is being paid, that means if they make a million dollars, the video's actually produced multi-millions of dollars in ad revenue.

Here are a list of YouTube Millionaires as reported by Forbes magazine in the 20 December 2016 issue.

Youtube name/channel	2016 Income
1. Pewdiepie	$15 Million

Makes video's of himself playing video games and making crude comments on girls dancing.

2. Atwood	$8 Million

YouTube Video Marketing Overview

Promotes products and tours with other Youtubers.

   3. Lilly Singh $7.5 Million

Makes comedy skits mostly featuring herself talking about her parents and relationship issues.

YouTube name/channel	2016 Income
4. Smosh	$7 Million

Comedy Duo.

5. Rosanna Pasino Nerdie Nummies $6 Million

Baking show

6. Markipler	$5.5 Million

Comments on Video Games.

7. German Garmendia	$5.5 Million

Got a publishing deal from his YouTube channel

8. Miranda Sings	$5 Million

Comedian

YouTube Video Marketing Overview

9. Collen Ballinger $5 Million

Comedian

10. Tyler Oakley $5 Million

Makes a diary. LGBT Activist

And these are just some the the top earners. There are many more making $50,000 a month talking about movies, how to put on make up or video taping a day at an amusement park.

A Few Keys to Video Marketing Success

1. Commitment

While many of the top YouTubers are funny, they take their business seriously. One of the first things you have to understand is that there is commitment needed to be successful on YouTube.

Many of the successful YouTubers put up video's daily! One such YouTuber is Grace Randolph (Beyond the Trailer). Grace comments on movie news and movie trailers. She typically uploads 3 video's a day.

YouTube Video Marketing Overview

2. Research

Just putting up a video will not guarantee views. You have to put in research for every video. Research if the topic is popular or trending. Research what keywords you should use in your video. Research the success of other video's. Skip the research, skip the success.

3. Popularity

There are certain topics on YouTube that are extremely popular. Star Wars, Disney, Scantily clad women, video games, comedy. Know the level of your topics popularity and try to use keyword planning to max out the highest possible level. Some educational material is extremely valuable, but not popular.

ZERO COST MARKETING OVERVIEW

This is a zero cost online marketing plan for any business, cause or idea you wish to promote. This plan will show you step by step how to use online marketing featuring YouTube and Article Marketing to get free advertising for this or any product. In addition, this report will show you how to use this zero cost marketing plan to create a passive income stream.

YouTube Video Marketing Overview

A Few Key Definitions

YouTube is a video-sharing website headquartered in San Bruno, California, United States. The service was created by three former PayPal employee in February 2005. In November 2006, it was bought by Google for 1.65 Billion dollars. According to the Huffington Post, YouTube has 1 billion active users each month. Or nearly one out of every two people on the internet.

AdSense (Google AdSense) is an advertising placement service by Google. The program is designed for website publishers who want to display targeted text, video or image advertisement on website pages and earn money when the site visitors view or click the ads.

Hyperlink is a link from a hypertext file or document to another location or file, typically activated by clicking on a highlighted word or image on the screen.

Black Hat

In search engine optimization (SEO) terminology, black hat SEO refers to the use of aggressive SEO strategies, techniques and tactics that focus only on search engines and not a human audience, and usually does not obey search engines guidelines.

YouTube Video Marketing Overview

Getting Started

You get started by opening up a YouTube account. Go to www.YouTube.com and follow the step by step instructions. Then you open up a AdSense account. The AdSense account will take about a week to open. AdSense is linked to your YouTube account and land bank account. AdSense will use your 9 digit routing number to deposit a small amount of money into your land bank account. You then have to report to AdSense the amount deposited. After the deposit is confirmed, AdSense will send you a postcard to verify your address. You must then report to AdSense the pin number locate on the postcard. Once all the verification takes place YouTube allows you to connect all of the accounts and by doing so, you can now monetize your video's and create a passive income stream.

Social Media

You should join Social Media web sites like Facebook, Google Plus, Digg, Twitter, Linkedin, Tumbler and Pinterest. Every time you upload a video. When you are finished Optimizing it, you should link it to all of your social media web sites. This creates Backlinks. A Backlink is an incoming hyperlink from one webpage to another. Google and YouTube will rank your video higher if it has a good number of Backlinks. However if you have too many, and it appears that you have created them artificially, then Google and YouTube can punish you by removing your video.

YouTube Video Marketing Overview

As long as you are backlinking organically and not using Black Hat software or Black Hat web sites, you should be find with Google and YouTube.

Show Me the Money!

Monetization involves you allowing AdSense to place ads that run before or are placed on your videos. If the ads are clicked on, you make money. If the ads are viewed in their entirety you make money.

After you have your accounts set up, you need to gather all of the tools you will be using to create videos. You can create your videos using a standard video camera and tripod and videotape yourself. Or any other number of ways you can capture video. However for this program we are going "zero cost" so there will be no need to purchase or obtain a video camera.

Getting Free Tools to Create Your Videos

We are going to use "Screen Capture" software. Go to http://screencast-o-matic.com/home to download a free screen capture software called Screencast-o-Matic. There are two versions. The Free version allows you to videotape up to 15 minutes of content and places a watermark on all of your recordings. The pro version makes longer recordings and has edit tools and not watermark. The pro version cost $15 and year and may be worth the investment once your business begins to make a profit.

YouTube Video Marketing Overview

Then next tool you will use in creating your videos is a free copy of the office software package called Apache OpenOffice. Go to https://www.openoffice.org/download/ to download the software.

100% Copyright Free Content

Now that you have to tools to create a video, you need content. Wikipedia is an excellent source of copyright free content, you can use to create your videos. There are many keyword phrases that you can use to find material. Later on in this book you will learn how to use the Google Ad Planner to get the best keyword phrases to use in your videos.

YouTube Video Marketing
SEO – The Key to Internet Riches

Search Engine Optimization

Analytics: Video Viewership

Through out this book I am going to discuss many YouTube analytics that factor into how your video is ranked in YouTube. Once someone clicks onto your video to view it, YouTube keeps track of how many minutes it was view. Videos that are viewed from beginning to end get ranked higher base on the belief that the content is good if the viewer keeps watching it. For this reason, it is usually a good idea to keep most your videos under five minutes. It addition, this allows you to create more videos to a related topic. It is better to have twenty 3 minute videos than one 1 hour video, because it is more likely that the 3 minute videos will be watched in their entirety. Also by creating 20 videos you now have 20 possible places for AdSense to place monetized ads and thus increase your earning potential 20 times.

Tags, Keywords and Keyword Phrases

Tags, keywords and keyword phrases are the most important part of getting your YouTube video to rank on the first page of YouTube. There is an old saying..."If you commit murder, where do you hide the body, where nobody will find it? On the second page of Google".

YouTube Video Marketing
SEO – The Key to Internet Riches

Although we are working on YouTube the principle is the same. You must rank on the first page of YouTube in order for your video to get views from standard YouTube web site traffic.

Keywords are words that relate to your video. Some keywords for business are:

Business, Marketing and Start-up

Keyword Phrases for business are:

how to make money from home, internet marketing, small business grants

Tags are Keywords or Keyword Phrases that you place on your YouTube video's editing page, in order to get viewers to find your video.

Your goal is to try to rank in the top 20(land on the first page of YouTube) for every or most of the Tags in your video.

Your Video Title

The title of your video should be a keyword phrase that you want to rank for. It should also be relevant to the content in the video. When your title, tags and description are all relevant it boosts your YouTube rankings.

YouTube Video Marketing
SEO – The Key to Internet Riches

Video Description

Each video is allowed to have a description. At the top of the description box, is where you should place a clickable or hyperlink, to either your web site or another video that you wish to viewer to see. Below the link should be a description of the video that contains content that is relative to the video. One short cut you can use it to cut and paste your video script into the description.

You video description should also have the keywords you used as tags. This adds to the videos relevancy.

You should also put links in you video to your social media addresses.

Half Time Adjustments

Any tags that are ranking your video in the top 20 should be placed in the headline/title of the video to boost their rank even higher.

One software that helps save you a tremendous amount of time doing this is called Tube Buddy.

https://www.tubebuddy.com/

YouTube Video Marketing
Writing Your Script

CREATING CONTENT

You have two options for creating content. On screen video of yourself using a digital camera or phone camera. Take notes of what you will discuss.

Know your topic before you hit record.

Recording Tips:

* Use good lighting.

* Try recording near a window during the day time.

* Limit background noise as much as possible.

* Use a POWERPOINT screen capture style video.

* Create bullet points

* Use free software like jing or camstudio to record it. You can also get a free 30 day trial of camtasia from TechSmith

* www.screencast-o-matic.com is another free solution.

* Use your computer's built in microphone.

YouTube Video Marketing
Writing Your Script

* Use a usb microphone is ideal, but not required.

* if you or kids have a usb gaming headset that works as well.

* most smart phones have a mp3 recording option.

Writing Your Script

Try to use words in your script that get and hold your viewers attention. Words like… you, want, now, free, limited time, All-American, imagine and how to, are just a few of the many words that are proven to stir a viewers emotions. Viewing a few copy writing videos on YouTube should help you to chose attention grabbing words.

AIDA is an acronym used in marketing and advertising that describes a common list of events that may occur when a consumer engages with an advertisement.

- A – attention (awareness): attract the attention of the customer.
- I – interest of the customer.
- D – desire: convince customers that they want and desire the product or service and that it will satisfy their needs.
- A – action: lead customers towards taking action and/or purchasing.

YouTube Video Marketing
Writing Your Script

Using a system like this gives one a general understanding of how to target a market effectively. Moving from step to step, one loses some percent of prospects.

AIDA is a historical model, rather than representing current thinking in the methods of advertising effectiveness.

A basic rule of thumb for writing your script is that one paragraph equals about 60 seconds of talking. So if you are trying to shoot a 3 minute video you what to create a 3 paragraph document for your script. Try to use words in our script that are relevant to the title of your video.

You can also cut and paste your script into a YouTube video editor, and make your video Closed Captioned. This will increase your rankings in the YouTube search engine and it will allow more people to understand your video and increase your views.

CREATING TOPICS FOR YOUR VIDEOS

It is time to brainstorm and write down topics for your videos.

Remember you could choose a video around your own information product if you had it.

YouTube Video Marketing
Writing Your Script

Get a notepad and think of 10 to 20 FAQ about your business.

http://answers.yahoo.com

Is a good source to find out what the potiential customers of your business are interested in.

Also look at articles on ezinearticles.com and see what topics come up the most for articles related to your business.

You can also browse forums related to your business.

Take a look at information products about your target market.

When you make a video that features Frequently Asked Questions each faq could be a short 1 to 3 minute video.

Use nichesuggest.com for a list of possible keyword ideas as well as seocentro and the google keyword planner.

Brainstorm 5 to 10 additional solution oriented videos. You should cover why the solution you are offering is better and why does your product recommendation solve your customer's problem.

YouTube Video Marketing
Writing Your Script

Try to think of every advantage possible. Read other reviews of similar products or businesses or view sales pages for ideas of content for your videos.

Creating a Multipurpose Close

There are certain things that you should say in almost all of your videos:

* Thank the viewer for watching

* Ask the viewer to Thumbs up or Like your video

* Ask the viewer to subscribe to your YouTube Channel

* Ask the viewer to leave a comment

* Ask the viewer to share your video link with friends or social media

YouTube Video Marketing
Writing Your Script

YOUR CALL TO ACTION

send your website visitors to a variety of places.

* A free website through weebly.com

* A free page through squidoo.com

* A free blog through blogspot.com

Use a tracking link like www.bit.ly or www.tinyurl.com

be careful as these links can change on you.

YouTube Video Marketing
Writing Your Script

UPLOADING VIDEO

Create your account at www.youtube.com you can use a google account if you have one already created. Upload your video. Then provide your keyword rich video title. Look at other examples of videos performing well in that space. Use keywords from your niche or business and topic research write a good description with the keywords in it.

Try to include at least 2 sentences in your description. More content in your description will not hurt you. Include your website link at the beginning of the description use format http://www.yourfreelink.com encourage likes, comments, or honest feedback at the end of the description. Make a call to action in the description as well.

Chapter 6
Best Way To Write A Business Plan

How to Write a Business Plan

Millions of people want to know what is the secret to making money. Most have come to the conclusion that it is to start a business. So how to start a business? The first thing you do to start is business is to create a business plan.

A business plan is a formal statement of a set of business goals, the reasons they are believed attainable, and the plan for reaching those goals. It may also contain background information about the organization or team attempting to reach those goals.

A professional business plan consists of eight parts.

1. Executive Summary

The executive summary is a very important part of your business plan. Many consider it the most important because it this part of your plan gives a summary of the current state of your business, where you want to take it and why the business plan you have made will be a success. When requesting funds to start your business, the executive summary is an chance to get the attention of a possible investor.

How to Write a Business Plan

2. Company Description

The company description part of your business plan gives a high level review of the different aspects of your business. This is like putting your elevator pitch into a brief summary that can help readers and possible investors quickly grasp the goal of your business and what will make it stand out, or what unique need it will fill.

3. Market Analysis

The market analysis part of your business plan should go into detail about your industries market and monetary potential. You should demonstrate detailed research with logical strategies for market penetration. Will you use low prices or high quality to penetrate the market?

4. Organization and Management

The Organization and Management section follows the Market Analysis. This part of the business plan will have your companies organizational structure, the type of business structure of incorporation, the ownership, management team and the qualifications of everyone holding these positions including the board of directors if necessary.

How to Write a Business Plan

5. Service or Product Line

The Service or Product Line part of your business plan gives you a chance to describe your service or product. Focus on the benefits to the customers more than what the product or service does. For example, a air conditioner makes cold air. The benefit of the product is it cools down and makes customers more comfortable whether they are driving in bumper to bumper traffic or a sick and sitting in a nursing home. Air Conditioners fill a need that could mean the difference between life and death. Use this section to state what are the most important benefits of your product or service and what need it fills.

6. Marketing and Sales

Having a proven marketing plan is essential element to the success of any business. Today online sales are dominating the marketplace. Present a strong internet marketing plan as well as social media plan. YouTube videos, Facebook Ads and Press Releases all can be part of your internet marketing plan. Passing out flyers and business cards are still an effective way to reach potential customers.

Use this part of your business plan to state your projected sales and how you came to that number. Do your research on similar companies for possible statistics on sales numbers.

How to Write a Business Plan

7. Funding Request

When you write your Funding Request section of your business plan, be sure to be detailed and have documentation of the cost of supplies, building space, transportation, overhead and promotion of your business.

8. Financial Projections

The following is a list of the important financial statements to include in your business plan packet.

Historical Financial Data

Your historical financial data would be bank statements, balance sheets and possible collateral for your loan.

Prospective Financial Data

The prospective financial data section of your business plan should show you potential growth within your industry, projecting out for at least the next five years.

You can have monthly or quarterly projections for the first year. Then project from year to year.

Include a ratio and trend analysis for all of your financial statements. Use colorful graphs to explain positive trends, as part of the financial projections section of your business plan.

How to Write a Business Plan

Appendix

The appendix should not be part of the main body of your business plan. It should only be provided on a need to know basis. Your business plan may be seen by a lot of people and you don't want certain information available to everybody. Lenders may need such information so you should have an appendix ready just in case.

The appendix would include:

Credit history (personal & business)

- Resumes of key managers
- Product pictures
- Letters of reference
- Details of market studies
- Relevant magazine articles or book references
- Licenses, permits or patents
- Legal documents
- Copies of leases

How to Write a Business Plan

    Building permits

    Contracts

    List of business consultants, including attorney and accountant

Keep a record of who you allow to see your business plan.

Include a Private Placement Disclaimer. A Private Placement Disclaimers is a private placement memorandum (PPM) is a document focused mainly on the possible downsides of an investment.

Chapter 7
Setting Goals
&
Staying Focused

Setting Goals & Staying Focused

1. Write it down.

"And the Lord answered me, and said, Write the vision, and make it plain upon tables, that he may run that readeth it."

Habakkuk 2:2   King James Version (KJV)

You must write down your goals in a place you can access them every day. This will help you to stay focus and better prioritize the things you have planned for any given day.

Keep an example of your vision. Maybe it's a photograph of a house you want to purchase or a video commercial of a car you want to own.

2. Put a date on it.

"Goals are dreams with a deadline."

Tony Robbins

Putting a date or deadline on your goals makes them more real and gives a sense of urgency to your actions. When you have a date of accomplishment set, it also helps you to stay focused and keep yourself honest to yourself and those you have told about the deadline.

Setting Goals & Staying Focused

3. List all the obstacles you have to overcome.

"Now no chastening for the present seemeth to be joyous, but grievous: nevertheless afterward it yieldeth the peaceable fruit of righteousness unto them which are exercised thereby."

Hebrews 12:11 King James Version

If it was easy, everybody would do it. There are going to be challenges. To the best of your ability, identify/exercise/educate yourself to those challenges and have a plan on how you will deal with them. Do not take a victim's mentality. Do this and after you overcome your challenges your success will yield a peaceable fruit.

"Life is a series of experiences, each one of which makes us bigger, even though sometimes it is hard to realize this. For the world was built to develop character, and we must learn that the setbacks and grieves which we endure help us in our marching onward."

Henry Ford

Setting Goals & Staying Focused

4. **Identify all the people, groups or organizations you will need to work with.**

"Know and accept that you can't do it all. You are one person and you alone will not solve all the problems in the sphere of life. Do what you can, nothing more, and say to yourself, "I've done the best I could today."

Tiffany Cooper

Get a team together to assist you. Delegate. There is a website call https://www.fiverr.com/ in which you can hire someone to do almost anything you need for a fee of $5 and currently a service fee of $1.

I have used this site frequently. If you decide to use fiverr use the rating system supplied and don't be shy about hiring more than one person to find the best qualified to do a job.

Setting Goals & Staying Focused

5. Spell out a Plan of Action.

"1 Blessed is the man that walketh not in the counsel of the ungodly, nor standeth in the way of sinners, nor sitteth in the seat of the scornful.

2 But his delight is in the law of the Lord; and in his law doth he meditate day and night.

3 And he shall be like a tree planted by the rivers of water, that bringeth forth his fruit in his season; his leaf also shall not wither; and whatsoever he doeth shall prosper."

Psalm 1 King James Version (KJV)

"and whatsoever he doeth shall prosper." You have to take ACTION!

Purchase a daily planner and write down a daily plan of action. Adjust if frequently if necessary. But have a plan of action written down, every day, to keep you focused and your mind from wandering.

6. Set a Time Limit.

Have a time limit for your actions. Other wise Analysis paralysis can set in.

Setting Goals & Staying Focused

7. Identify all of the Benefits of Achieving your Goal.

"10 The thief cometh not, but for to steal, and to kill, and to destroy: I am come that they might have life, and that they might have it more abundantly."

John 10:10 King James Version (KJV)

Envision and list all of the benefits of achieving your goals. Having a successful business could give you...

* More time to spend with your family

* Provide better health care for you & your family

* Take the vacations you always wanted

Whatevery the benefits are, write them down, imagine them, if possible cut out a photo of them.

Just about every building on the planet was build at least twice. First in someone's mind, and then constructed. Build your desires in you mind. Then watch them materialize.

"11 Now faith is the substance of things hoped for, the evidence of things not seen."

Hebrews 11:1   King James Version (KJV)

Chapter 8

REAL ESTATE TERMS

REAL ESTATE TERMS

Acceleration Clause - A contract provision that allows a lender to require a borrower to repay all or part of an outstanding loan if certain requirements are not met. An acceleration clause outlines the reasons that the lender can demand loan repayment. Also known as "acceleration covenant".

Accrued Depreciation - Depreciation is the loss in value to any structure due to a variety of factors, such as wear and tear, age, and poor location. The term accrued depreciation means the total depreciation of a building from all causes.

Accrued Interest - In finance, accrued interest is the interest on a bond or loan that has accumulated since the principal investment, or since the previous coupon payment if there has been one already. For a financial instrument such as a bond, interest is calculated and paid in set intervals (for instance annually or semi-annually).

Active Income - Active income is income for which services have been performed. This includes wages, tips, salaries, commissions and income from businesses in which there is material participation.

REAL ESTATE TERMS

Add-on Interest - A method of calculating interest whereby the interest payable is determined at the beginning of a loan and added onto the principal. The sum of the interest and principal is the amount repayable upon maturity.

Adjustable Rate Mortgage (ARM) - A variable-rate mortgage, adjustable-rate mortgage (ARM), or tracker mortgage is a mortgage loan with the interest rate on the note periodically adjusted based on an index which reflects the cost to the lender of borrowing on the credit markets.

Cash flow after taxes (CFAT) - Cash flow after taxes (CFAT) is a measure of financial performance that looks at the company's ability to generate cash flow through its operations. It is calculated by adding back non-cash accounts such as amortization, depreciation, restructuring costs and impairments to net income.

Agent - One who is legally authorized to act on behalf of another person.

Agreement for sale - An agreement of sale constitutes the terms and conditions of sale of a property by the seller to the buyer. ... Sale deed is the document prepared at the time of full payment made by the buyer and when the actual transfer of the property takes place.

REAL ESTATE TERMS

Alienation clause - A clause in a mortgage contract that requires full payment of the balance of a mortgage at the lender's discretion if the property is sold or the title to the property changes to another person. Nearly all mortgages have an alienation clause.

All-inclusive deed of trust (AITD) - An All Inclusive Trust Deed (AITD) is a new deed of trust that includes the balance due on the existing note plus new funds advanced; also known as a wrap-around mortgage.

American Land Title Association (ALTA) -The American Land Title Association (ALTA) is a trade association representing the title insurance industry. Founded in 1907, ALTA also focuses on a property's abstract of title, which ties the history of the title to a particular piece of real estate.

Amortization - Amortization is an accounting term that refers to the process of allocating the cost of an intangible asset over a period of time. It also refers to the repayment of loan principal over time.

Amortized loan - An amortized loan is a loan with scheduled periodic payments that consist of both principal and interest. An amortized loan payment pays the relevant interest expense for the period before any principal is paid and reduced.

REAL ESTATE TERMS

Appraisal - an expert estimate of the value of something.

Appraised value - An appraised value is an evaluation of a property's value based on a given point in time that is performed by a professional appraiser during the mortgage origination process. The appraiser is usually chosen by the lender, but the appraisal is paid for by the borrower.

Appraiser - A practitioner who has the knowledge and expertise necessary to estimate the value of an asset, or the likelihood of an event occurring, and the cost of such an occurrence.

Arbitration - the use of an arbitrator to settle a dispute.

Arbitration clause - An arbitration clause is a clause in a contract that requires the parties to resolve their disputes through an arbitration process

Asking price - the price at which something is offered for sale.

Assessment - the evaluation or estimation of the nature, quality, or ability of someone or something.

Assignee - a person to whom a right or liability is legally transferred.

REAL ESTATE TERMS

Assignment - An assignment (Latin cessio) is a term used with similar meanings in the law of contracts and in the law of real estate. In both instances, it encompasses the transfer of rights held by one party—the assignor—to another party—the assignee.

Assumption Clause - A provision in a mortgage contract that allows the seller of a home to pass responsibility to the buyer of the home for the existing mortgage. In other words, the new homeowner assumes the existing mortgage. There are typically many conditions and a fee required in an assumption clause.

Assumption of mortgage - Mortgage assumption is the conveyance of the terms and balance of an existing mortgage to the purchaser of a financed property, commonly requiring that the assuming party is qualified under lender or guarantor guidelines.

At-risk rule - Tax laws limiting the amount of losses an investor (usually a limited partner) can claim. Only the amount actually at risk can be deducted.

REAL ESTATE TERMS

Authorization to sell - Authorization to sell is a listing contract whereby a representative is employed by a seller to secure a buyer for the property. An authorization to sell does not give the agent the authority to enter into a binding contract of sale.

Backup offer - A backup offer is when a home seller has accepted an offer from a buyer, but is still accepting offers from other buyers. Sellers state that they are accepting backup offers if they think the current offer may fall through

Balloon mortgage - a mortgage in which a large portion of the borrowed principal is repaid in a single payment at the end of the loan period.

Balloon payment - a repayment of the outstanding principal sum made at the end of a loan period, interest only having been paid hitherto.

Binder insurance - binder. A legal agreement issued by either an agent or an insurer to provide temporary evidence of insurance until a policy can be issued. Binders should contain definite time limits, should be in writing, and should clearly designate the insurer with which the risk is bound

Capital gain - a profit from the sale of property or of an investment.

REAL ESTATE TERMS

Capitalization - the provision of capital for a company, or the conversion of income or assets into capita

Cash basis taxpayer - A taxpayer who reports income and deductions in the year that they are actually paid or received. Cash basis taxpayers cannot report receivables as income, nor deduct promissory notes as payments.

Cash flow - the total amount of money being transferred into and out of a business, especially as affecting liquidity.

Certificate of title - A certificate of title is a state or municipal-issued document that identifies the owner or owners of personal or real property. A certificate of title provides documentary evidence of the right of ownership.

Chattel - an item of property other than real estate.

Closing costs - Closing costs are fees paid at the closing of a real estate transaction. This point in time called the closing is when the title to the property is conveyed (transferred) to the buyer. Closing costs are incurred by either the buyer or the seller.

REAL ESTATE TERMS

Cloud on title - Any document, claim, unreleased lien or encumbrance that might invalidate or impair the title to real property or make the title doubtful. Clouds on title are usually discovered during a title search. Clouds on title are resolved through initiating a quitclaim deed or a commencement of action to quiet title.

Co-insurance - a type of insurance in which the insured pays a share of the payment made against a claim.

Collateral - something pledged as security for repayment of a loan, to be forfeited in the event of a default.

Commission - A fee charged by a broker or agent for his/her service in facilitating a transaction, such as the buying or selling of securities or real estate. In the case of securities trading, brokers can be split into two broad categories depending on the commissions they charge.

Contract of sale - A real estate contract is a contract between parties for the purchase and sale, exchange, or other conveyance of real estate.

REAL ESTATE TERMS

Cost approach - Cost approach. ... The fundamental premise of the cost approach is that a potential user of real estate won't, or shouldn't, pay more for a property than it would cost to build an equivalent. The cost of construction minus depreciation, plus land, therefore is a limit, or at least a metric, of market value.

Debt coverage ratio - In corporate finance, DSCR refers to the amount of cash flow available to meet annual interest and principal payments on debt, including sinking fund payments. In personal finance, DSCR refers to a ratio used by bank loan officers in determining debt servicing ability.

Declining balance method - A declining balance method is a common depreciation-calculation system that involves applying the depreciation rate against the non-depreciated balance.

Deed - A deed (anciently "an evidence") is any legal instrument in writing which passes, affirms or confirms an interest, right, or property and that is signed, attested, delivered, and in some jurisdictions, sealed. It is commonly associated with transferring (conveyancing) title to property.

REAL ESTATE TERMS

Deed of trust - In real estate in the United States, a deed of trust or trust deed is a deed wherein legal title in real property is transferred to a trustee, which holds it as security for a loan (debt) between a borrower and lender. The equitable title remains with the borrower.

Depreciation - Depreciation is an accounting method of allocating the cost of a tangible asset over its useful life. Businesses depreciate long-term assets for both tax and accounting purposes.

Double escrow - Double escrow. ... Double escrow is a set of real estate transactions involving two contracts of sale for the same property, to two different back-to-back buyers, at the same or two different prices, arranged to close on the same day.

Due diligence - Due diligence means taking caution, performing calculations, reviewing documents, procuring insurance, walking the property, etc. — essentially doing your homework for the property BEFORE you actually make the purchase

REAL ESTATE TERMS

Earnest money - Earnest money is a deposit made to a seller showing the buyer's good faith in a transaction. Often used in real estate transactions, earnest money allows the buyer additional time when seeking financing. Earnest money is typically held jointly by the seller and buyer in a trust or escrow account.

Eminent domain - Eminent Domain. The power of the government to take private property and convert it into public use. The Fifth Amendment provides that the government may only exercise this power if they provide just compensation to the property owners.

Encroachment - A situation in real estate where a property owner violates the property rights of his neighbor by building something on the neighbor's land or by allowing something to hang over onto the neighbor's property.

Equity participation - Equity participation is the ownership of shares in a company or property. ... The greater the equity participation rate, the higher the percentage of shares owned by stakeholders. Allowing stakeholders to own shares ties the stakeholders' success with that of the company or real estate investment.

REAL ESTATE TERMS

Escrow - Escrow generally refers to money held by a third-party on behalf of transacting parties. ... It is best known in the United States in the context of real estate (specifically in mortgages where the mortgage company establishes an escrow account to pay property tax and insurance during the term of the mortgage).

Escrow instructions - n. the written instructions by buyer and seller of real estate given to a title company, escrow company or individual escrow in "closing" a real estate transaction. These instructions are generally prepared by the escrow holder and then approved by the parties and their agents. (See: closing, escrow)

Estoppel - Estoppel Certificate. An estoppel certificate is a document used in mortgage negotiations to establish facts and financial obligations, such as outstanding amounts due that can affect the settlement of a loan. It is required by a lender of a third party in a real estate transaction

Exclusive right to sell listing - An Exclusive Right to Sell/Lease means that the listing brokerage has an exclusive listing agreement with the Seller. (Sorry about using a word in the term to define the term!) It means that a commission would be owed to the Listing Brokerage when the property is sold to a buyer, regardless of who brings the buyer.

REAL ESTATE TERMS

Fair market value - The fair market value is the price at which the property would change hands between a willing buyer and a willing seller, neither being under any compulsion to buy or to sell and both having reasonable knowledge of relevant facts.

Fee simple - In English law, a fee simple or fee simple absolute is an estate in land, a form of freehold ownership. It is a way that real estate may be owned in common law countries, and is the highest possible ownership interest that can be held in real property.

First right of refusal - A right of first refusal is a contractual right granted by an owner of property. The owner gives the holder of the right an opportunity to enter into a business transaction with the owner according to specified terms, before the owner may enter into that transaction with a third party.

Foreclosure - Foreclosure is a legal process in which a lender attempts to recover the balance of a loan from a borrower, who has stopped making payments to the lender, by forcing the sale of the asset used as the collateral for the loan.

REAL ESTATE TERMS

Gift deed - Quitclaim Deed Vs. Gift Deed. Property deeds define and protect ownership in a home. In real estate, deeds are legal documents that transfer ownership of a property from one party to another. ... Each type of deed is used for a specific situation.

Grantee - In real estate, the grantee is the recipient of a property - the person who will be taking title, as named in the the legal document used to transfer the real estate. The person who is relinquishing the property is called the grantor.

Grantor - First, it's important to review the legal definition of "grantor" and "grantee." In a real estate transaction, the grantor is the party that conveys the property in question. The grantor may be an individual, business entity or partnership. The grantee is the party that receives the property

Gross income - A real estate investment term, Gross Operating Income refers to the result of subtracting the credit and vacancy losses from a property's gross potential income. Also Known As: Effective Gross Income (EGI)

Gross rent multiplier - Gross Rent Multiplier is the ratio of the price of a real estate investment to its annual rental income before accounting for expenses such as property taxes, insurance, utilities, etc.

REAL ESTATE TERMS

Highest and best use - The Appraisal Institute defines highest and best use as follows: The reasonably probable and legal use of vacant land or an improved property that is physically possible, appropriately supported, financially feasible, and that results in the highest value.

Income approach to value - The income approach is a real estate appraisal method that allows investors to estimate the value of a property by taking the net operating income of the rent collected and dividing it by the capitalization rate.

Installment sale - A method of sale that allows for partial deferral of any capital gain to future taxation years. Installment sales require the buyer to make regular payments, or installments, on an annual basis, plus interest if installment payments are to be made in subsequent taxation years.

Insurable title - Marketable Title vs. Insurable Title. ... When a title is marketable it means that the chain of ownership (title) to a particular piece of property is clear and free from defects. And as such, it can be marketed for sale without additional effort by the seller or potential buyer.

REAL ESTATE TERMS

Interest - Estates and ownership interests defined. The law recognizes different sorts of interests, called estates, in real property. The type of estate is generally determined by the language of the deed, lease, bill of sale, will, land grant, etc., through which the estate was acquired.

Internal rate of return (IRR) - Internal rate of return (IRR) is a metric used in capital budgeting measuring the profitability of potential investments. Internal rate of return is a discount rate that makes the net present value (NPV) of all cash flows from a particular project equal to zero. ... r = discount rate, and. t = number of time periods

Involuntary lien - involuntary lien. A lien on real estate that results without the property owners' voluntary cooperation in the placement of the lien. Examples include tax liens and judgment liens. Contrast with a mortgage,which is voluntary.

Joint and several note - Joint and several note is a promissory note which is the note of all and of each of the makers as to its legal obligation between the parties to it.

REAL ESTATE TERMS

Joint tenancy - A type of property right where two or more people own or rent a property together, each with equal rights and obligations, until one owner dies. Upon an owner's death, that owner's interest in the property passes to the survivors without the property having to go through probate.

Judgment proof - People are judgment-proof if they lack the resources or insurance to pay a court judgment against them. For example, suppose that a thief steals your car, sells it, and then burns all of his worldly possessions. Even if you sued him and won, you could not recover anything because the thief is judgment-proof.

Lease option - A lease option (more formally Lease With the Option to Purchase) is a type of contract used in both residential and commercial real estate. In a lease-option, a property owner and tenant agree that, at the end of a specified rental period for a given property, the renter has the option of purchasing the property.

Letter of credit - 1. INTRODUCTION. Letters of credit are often used in real estate transactions to secure obligations. ... For example, a tenant may request its bank to issue a letter of credit to the landlord as security. In such a transaction, the tenant is the applicant, the bank is the issuer and the landlord is the beneficiary.

REAL ESTATE TERMS

Leverage - Leverage is the use of various financial instruments or borrowed capital to increase the potential return of an investment – and it is an extremely common term on both Wall Street and in the Main Street real estate market. (Learn more about the various uses of leverage in Leveraged Investment Showdown.)

Like kind property - Like-Kind Property. Any two assets or properties that are considered to be the same type, making an exchange between them tax free. To qualify as like kind, two assets must be of the same type (e.g. two pieces of residential real estate), but do not have to be of the same quality.

Limited partnership - RELP' A limited partnership entity organized to invest in real estate. A Real Estate Limited Partnership is typically organized with an experienced property manager or real estate development firm serving as the general partner.

Lis pendens - In United States law, a lis pendens is a written notice that a lawsuit has been filed concerning real estate, involving either the title to the property or a claimed ownership interest in it.

REAL ESTATE TERMS

Loan to value - The loan to value or LTV ratio of a property is the percentage of the property's value that is mortgaged. ... Loan to Value is used in commercial real estate as well. Examples: $300,000 appraised value of a home. $240,000 mortgage on the property. $240,000 / $300,000 = .80 or 80% Loan to Value Ratio

Market value - Market value is the most probable price that a property should bring in a competitive and open market under all conditions requisite to a fair sale, the buyer and seller, each acting prudently, knowledgeably and assuming the price is not affected by undue stimulus.

Mechanics lien - A guarantee of payment to builders, contractors and construction firms that build or repair structures. Mechanic's liens also extend to suppliers of materials and subcontractors and cover building repairs as well.

Mortgage broker - A mortgage broker is an intermediary working with a borrower and a lender while qualifying the borrower for a mortgage. The broker gathers income, asset and employment documentation, a credit report and other information for assessing the borrower's ability to secure financing.

REAL ESTATE TERMS

Multiple listing - A multiple listing service (MLS, also multiple listing system or multiple listings service) is a suite of services that real estate brokers use to establish contractual offers of compensation (among brokers) and accumulate and disseminate information to enable appraisals.

Net income - Net operating income (NOI) is a calculation used to analyze real estate investments that generate income. Net operating income equals all revenue from the property minus all reasonably necessary operating expenses

Net rentable area - Actual square-unit of a building that may be leased or rented to tenants, the area upon which the lease or rental payments are computed. It usually excludes common areas, elevator shafts, stairways, and space devoted to cooling, heating, or other equipment. Also called net leasable area.

Non-recourse note - Nonrecourse debt or a nonrecourse loan is a secured loan (debt) that is secured by a pledge of collateral, typically real property, but for which the borrower is not personally liable.

REAL ESTATE TERMS

Obsolescence - Functional obsolescence is a reduction in the usefulness or desirability of an object because of an outdated design feature, usually one that cannot be easily changed. The term is commonly used in real estate, but has a wide application.

Option - A real estate purchase option is a contract on a specific piece of real estate that allows the buyer the exclusive right to purchase the property. Once a buyer has an option to buy a property, the seller cannot sell the property to anyone else.

Passive activity income - Internal Revenue Service (IRS) defines two types of passive activity: trade or business activities not materially participated in, and rental activities even if the taxpayer materially participated in them (unless the taxpayer is a real estate professional).

Point - In real estate mortgages, a point refers to the origination fee charged by the lender, with each point being equal to 1% of the amount of the loan. It can also refer to each percentage difference between a mortgage's interest rate and the prime interest rate.

Possession - A principle of real estate law that allows a person who possesses someone else's land for an extended period of time to claim legal title to that land.

REAL ESTATE TERMS

Potential gross income - The amount of income produced by a piece of property, plus miscellaneous income, less vacancy costs and collection losses. Effective gross income is a metric commonly used to evaluate the value of a piece of investment property. ... The EGI for the property is $500,000 - $100,000, or $400,000.

Preliminary title report - A preliminary title sets forth various details about a piece of real estate, including: Ownership;

   Liens and encumbrances; and Easements.

The information in a preliminary title report, also known as a title search, is gathered from the property records in the county where the property is located.

Prepayment penalty - Prepayment Penalty. A prepayment penalty is a clause in a mortgage contract stating that a penalty will be assessed if the mortgage is prepaid within a certain time period. The penalty is based on a percentage of the remaining mortgage balance or a certain number of months' worth of interest.

Principal - In commercial law, a principal is a person, legal or natural, who authorizes an agent to act to create one or more legal relationships with a third party.

REAL ESTATE TERMS

Pro forma - What does 'Pro Forma' mean. Pro forma, a Latin term, literally means "for the sake of form" or "as a matter of form." In the world of investing, pro forma refers to a method by which financial results are calculated. This method of calculation places emphasis on present or projected figures.

Promissory note - In the United States, a mortgage note (also known as a real estate lien note, borrower's note) is a promissory note secured by a specified mortgage loan; it is a written promise to repay a specified sum of money plus interest at a specified rate and length of time to fulfill the promise.

Property management - Property management is the operation, control, and oversight of real estate as used in its most broad terms. Management indicates a need to be cared for, monitored and accountability given for its useful life and condition.

Quit claim deed - A quitclaim deed is a legal instrument which is used to transfer interest in real property. The entity transferring its interest is called the grantor, and when the quitclaim deed is properly completed and executed, it transfers any interest the grantor has in the property to a recipient, called the grantee.

REAL ESTATE TERMS

Real estate owned (REO) - Real estate owned or REO is a term used in the United States to describe a class of property owned by a lender—typically a bank, government agency, or government loan insurer—after an unsuccessful sale at a foreclosure auction.

Real property - Real estate is "property consisting of land and the buildings on it, along with its natural resources such as crops, minerals or water; immovable property of this nature; an interest vested in this (also) an item of real property, (more generally) buildings or housing in general.

Realized gain - The amount by which the sale price of an asset exceeds its purchase price. Unless the realized gain came from a tax-exempt or tax-deferred asset, it is taxable. However, the type of taxation to which it is subject varies according to how long the asset has been owned. A realized gain from an asset owned longer than one year is usually taxed at the capital gains rate, while an asset owned for a period shorter than a year is often subject to the higher income tax rate. It is also called the recognized gain.

REAL ESTATE TERMS

Refinancing - Getting a new mortgage to replace the original is called refinancing. Refinancing is done to allow a borrower to obtain a better interest term and rate. The first loan is paid off, allowing the second loan to be created, instead of simply making a new mortgage and throwing out the original mortgage.

Rental concession - Rental Concessions are benefits that are offered by the landlord to his tenants. Concessions are usually offered to draw tenants to vacant properties. Some other landlords may choose to offer a concession if the tenant decides to renew the lease. Even when the landlord is planning to sell a home, in return for his tenants co-operation he may offer incentives or concessions.

Replacement cost - A replacement cost is the cost to replace an asset of a company at the same or equal value, and the asset to be replaced could be a building, investment securities, accounts receivable or liens.

Reproduction cost - The costs involved with identically reproducing an asset or property with the same materials and specifications as an insured property based on current prices.

REAL ESTATE TERMS

Rescission - Rescission is the cancellation of a real estate contract between the buyer and seller. The act of rescinding a contract will "unwind" the transaction specified in the contract. A real estate contract may be rescinded at varying points during a transaction.

Restrictive covenant - A restrictive covenant is any type of agreement that requires the buyer to either take or abstain from a specific action. In real estate transactions, restrictive covenants are binding legal obligations written into the deed of a property by the seller.

Right of survivorship - The right of survivorship is an attribute of several types of joint ownership of property, most notably joint tenancy and tenancy in common. When jointly owned property includes a right of survivorship, the surviving owner automatically absorbs a dying owner's share of the property. Thus if A and B jointly own a house with a right of survivorship, and B dies, A becomes the sole owner of the house, despite any contrary intent in B's will.

REAL ESTATE TERMS

Secondary mortgage market - A secondary mortgage market is the market where mortgage loans and servicing rights are bought and sold between mortgage originators, mortgage aggregators (securitizers) and investors. The secondary mortgage market is extremely large and liquid.

Short-rate - The relatively higher insurance premium rate charged for coverage when one cancels a policy earlier than originally agreed upon. Rather than receiving a pro rata refund of the unearned premium, the property owner receives a smaller amount.

Standby commitment - A standby commitment is a formal agreement by a bank agreeing to lend money to a borrower up to a specified amount for a specific period. It is also known as firm commitment lending. The amount given under standby commitment is to be used only in specified contingency.

Subject to mortgage - circumstance in which a buyer takes title to mortgaged real property but is not personally liable for the payment of the amount due. The buyer must make payments in order to keep the property; however, with default, only the buyer's equity in that property is lost. Contrast assumption of mortgage.

REAL ESTATE TERMS

Subordination - For an individual, the most frequent example of a subordination agreement is when an individual attempts to refinance the first mortgage on a property which has a second mortgage. The second mortgage has a lower priority than the first mortgage, but these priorities may be upset by refinancing the loan.

Supply and demand - The law of supply and demand is a basic economic principle that explains the relationship between supply and demand for a good or service and how the interaction affects the price of that good or service. The relationship of supply and demand affects the housing market and the price of a house

Tax lien - A tax lien is a lien imposed by law upon a property to secure the payment of taxes. A tax lien may be imposed for delinquent taxes owed on real property or personal property, or as a result of failure to pay income taxes or other taxes.

Tax shelter -Tax shelters can range from investments or investment accounts that provide favorable tax ... evasion, the illegal avoidance of taxes through misrepresentation or similar means. ... A tax shelter product designed to create large, seemingly real .

REAL ESTATE TERMS

Tenancy by entirety - Tenants by entirety (TBE) is a method in some states by which married couples can hold the title to a property. In order for one spouse to modify his or her interest in the property in any way, the consent of both spouses is required by tenants by entirety.

Tenants-in-common - Tenancy in common is a type of shared ownership of property, where each owner owns a share of the property. Unlike in a joint tenancy, these shares can be of unequal size, and can be freely transferred to other owners both during life and via a will.

Title - a right or claim to the ownership of property or to a rank or throne.

Title insurance policy - Title insurance is an insurance policy that covers the loss of ownership interest in a property due to legal defects and is required if the property is under mortgage. The most common type of title insurance is a lender's title insurance, which is paid for by the borrower but protects only the lender.

Trust deed - a deed of conveyance creating and setting out the conditions of a trust

Usury - the illegal action or practice of lending money at unreasonably high rates of interest.

REAL ESTATE TERMS

Vacancy and rent loss - Vacancy and Credit Loss in real estate investing is the amount of money or percentage of net operating income that is estimated to not be realized due to non-payment of rents and vacant units

Vacancy factor - The vacancy rate is the percentage of all available units in a rental property, such as a hotel or apartment complex, that are vacant or unoccupied at a particular time. It is the opposite of the occupancy rate, which is the percentage of units in a rental property that are occupied.

Warranty deed - a deed that guarantees a clear title to the buyer of real property.

Will - A will or testament is a legal document by which a person, the testator, expresses their wishes as to how their property is to be distributed at death, and names one or more persons, the executor, to manage the estate until its final distribution.

Without recourse - a formula used to disclaim responsibility for future nonpayment, especially of a negotiable financial instrument.

Wrap-around - "wrap", is a form of secondary financing for the purchase of real property. The seller extends to the buyer a junior mortgage which wraps around and exists in addition to any superior mortgages already secured by the property.

Please Leave a Great Review!

I have purchased all of the top real estate investing books on the market, and most have a handful of out dated web sites for their sources of properties.

There is not another real estate investing book on the market that gives you as many sources for wholesale real estate than this book.

My book gives you more and in most cases for less!

I have enjoyed doing all the research and sharing my real world real estate investing experience in what I hope is easy to understand terminology.

So I ask you to leave a honest and hopefully great review!

Thank you. Warm Regards,

Christian Mahoney

Amazon Review

Get Massive Money for Real Estate Now!

1. Private Lending and Hard Money (Text Manual) (similar guides have sold for $1,500.00 alone)

2. Real Estate Investing Guide (Text Guide)

3. Goldmine Government Grants (Video Training Program)

4. Residential Government Grant Programs (Video Training Program)

5. Commercial Government Grant Programs (Video Training Program)

6. Creative Financing (Video Training Program)

7. Expert Credit Repair (Video Training Program)

8. Million Dollar Video Marketing (Video Training Program)

9. Customer List Building (Video Training Program)

10. Massive Web Site Traffic (Video Training Program)

11. SEO Marketing (Video Training Program)

12. Bonus 1000 Package!!!

Just Hit the Link Below Right Now!!!

Don't Wait....You'll Wait Your Life Away...

http://www.BrianSMahoney.com

Get Our Massive Money Complete Internet Marketing Video Training Program at:

(Zero Cost Internet Marketing complete 142 video series)

$1,997 Megasized Money Making Marketing Program

ONLY $67 !!!!

https://goo.gl/Qed1dY

**Join Our VIP Mailing List and Get FREE Money Making Training Videos! Then Start Making Money within 24 hours!
Plus if you join our Mailing list you can get Revised and New Edition versions of your book free!**

And Notifications of other FREE Offers!

Just Hit/Type in the Link Below

https://mahoneyproducts.wixsite.com/win1

www.ingramcontent.com/pod-product-compliance
Lightning Source LLC
Chambersburg PA
CBHW070302230526
45470CB00002B/680